SKILL SHARPENERS
Science
1

Contents

Space and Earth Science

Environment and Ecology Science

Engineering and Design

How to Use This Book

Learning About Science

Science is all around us, and children are naturally curious about their world. They investigate, problem solve, experiment, and imagine new ways to do things—they are, by nature, scientists! Studies show that children learn best through hands-on experiences. As your child asks questions about the world, you may look to science to answer some of those questions. This book will help you connect your child's real-world experiences to science concepts and vocabulary.

The lessons in this book provide information and activities about physical, life, and earth sciences in addition to science and engineering careers.

Reading Selections

Read the selection to your child. Point to vocabulary words and have your child say each word aloud. Discuss how the illustrations or photos help your child better understand the science concept. Then, if your child is able, have him or her read the selection to you.

Visual Literacy

Illustrations and photos help your child relate science concepts to the real-world. Use the visual literacy activities to reinforce the science concepts that were presented in the reading selection. Provide your child with support by reading the directions aloud and answering any questions he or she may have about the activity.

Vocabulary

The vocabulary activities range from word puzzles to writing vocabulary words to complete sentences. Provide your child with support by reading the directions aloud and answering any questions he or she may have about the activity.

Hands-on Activities

The hands-on activities provide your child with opportunities to connect science concepts to the real-world. The activities focus on developing process skills such as observing, collecting, and organizing information. In addition, you and your child will create projects that bring science concepts to life. These activities are designed for parents and children to complete together.

Concept:

Sound can make objects vibrate, and vibrations make sound.

Vibrations Make Sound

Boom, boom, boom!
That's the sound of a drum.
Where does sound come from?
Sound comes from vibrations .

When you hit the top of the drum, it will vibrate, or move over and over very fast.

As the drum vibrates,
it makes sound waves that
move through the air.

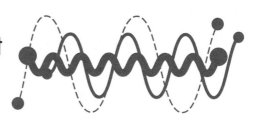

Some sound waves
are musical .

Sound

Physical Science

We **pluck**
some instruments
to make sound.

We **blow**
some instruments
to make sound.

We **hit**
some instruments
to make sound.

We **shake**
some instruments
to make sound.

Physical Science

Skill:

Match graphic images to science concepts

Sound Match

Draw a line to match.

sound waves

musical

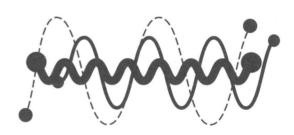

vibrations

Finish the sentence.

Sound comes from _____.

Sound

Making Sound

Draw a line to match.

hit

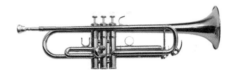

pluck

blow

shake

Sound

Physical Science

Sound Words

Read the words in the word box.
Find the hidden words. Circle them.

Word Box

pluck	hit	vibrations	musical
shake	blow	sound	move

```
v  i  b  r  a  t  i  o  n  s
b  l  a  m  v  r  c  h  p  w
x  m  u  s  i  c  a  l  l  v
h  v  d  c  t  s  o  u  u  a
i  a  s  h  a  k  e  a  c  e
t  m  o  o  l  c  e  v  k  s
u  o  s  e  b  n  n  l  p  o
d  v  v  i  b  l  o  w  e  u
m  e  c  r  k  e  v  l  t  n
b  a  i  o  n  w  i  v  a  d
```

Physical Science

Skill Sharpeners—Science • EMC 5321 • © Evan-Moor Corp.

Use Vocabulary

Finish each sentence.

| vibrates | move | sound |

1. When you hit a drum, it _____.

2. The vibrations make _____.

3. Sound waves _____ through the air.

Draw an instrument you **blow** to make sound.

Physical Science

Listen to Vibrations

Use objects from your house to make sounds.

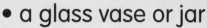
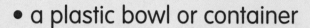

What You Need

Set 1

- a wooden spoon
- a fork
- your hand

Set 2

- a glass vase or jar
- a plastic bowl or container
- a metal pan

What You Do

1 Use each item in Set 1 to tap lightly on an item from Set 2. Notice how the vibrations you create make a different sound for each object.

2 Draw an X in the chart after you try each item.

wooden spoon	◯ glass	◯ metal	◯ plastic
fork	◯ glass	◯ metal	◯ plastic
hand	◯ glass	◯ metal	◯ plastic

Sound

Skill Sharpeners—Science • EMC 5321 • © Evan-Moor Corp.

Making Sounds

Put objects into a cup and shake it up!

What You Need

- an empty paper cup with a lid
- objects that fit inside the cup: uncooked rice or beans, coins, boardgame pieces, cotton balls, cord or yarn, etc.

What You Do

1 Put one group of objects inside the cup. Place the lid on the cup and shake it up. Listen to the sound.

2 Empty the cup and put a different group of objects in it. Repeat until you have experimented with all the objects.

3 Draw which objects made loud or quiet sounds.

These made a **loud** sound.	These made a **quiet** sound.

Physical Science

Concept:

There are different sources of light.

Light

Light is all around us.

Some light comes from nature.

sun

moon

stars

Some light comes from things that people make.

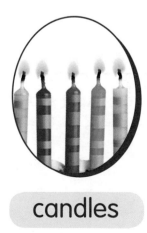
candles

flashlight

lamp

Light helps us see.
If we did not have light,
the world would be dark.

Light helps us live.
People, animals, and
plants need light.

Skill:

Match graphic images to words

Light Match

Draw a line to match.

candle

sun

lamp

moon

Finish the sentence.

Light helps us _____.

Who Makes It?

Skill:

Match graphic images to science concepts

Look at the picture. Check the correct box.

nature

people

nature ⃝   people ⃝

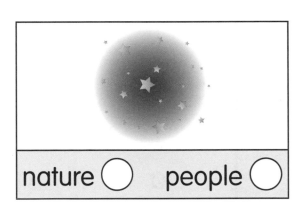

nature ⃝   people ⃝

nature ⃝   people ⃝

nature ⃝   people ⃝

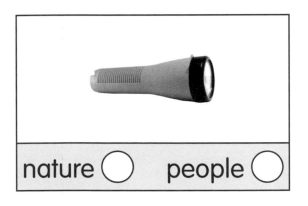

nature ⃝   people ⃝

nature ⃝   people ⃝

Light

Skills:

Read science words; Visual discrimination

Light Words

Read the words in the word box.
Find the hidden words. Circle them.

Word Box

nature	light	live	dark
moon	stars	lamp	candle

```
l  i  n  d  m  o  o  n  k  a
f  g  c  e  s  d  l  h  n  l
e  l  a  m  p  o  i  s  g  i
c  h  n  a  t  u  r  e  t  v
a  t  r  k  i  d  m  f  s  e
n  a  l  i  g  h  t  e  l  k
d  g  s  f  v  i  n  t  d  a
l  n  d  a  r  k  d  v  e  o
e  l  a  o  b  s  t  a  r  s
```

Physical Science

Use Vocabulary

Finish each sentence.

| light | nature | live |

1. Some light comes from _____.

2. If we did not have _____, the world would be dark.

3. Light helps us _____.

Draw light that comes from nature.

Lights Inside

Your house has light from things that people made. Draw four lights that people made and write the names.

Light

Lights Outside

You can see light from nature outside. Draw three sources of light from nature and write the names.

Skill:

Apply science concepts to real-world situations

Concept:

Shadows are produced when a light source is blocked.

Light and Shadows

Light moves in a line.

Light can move through some things.

Light moves through glass.

Light cannot move through other things.

Light does not move through a ball.

When light cannot move through something, you may see a shadow .

A shadow is a dark spot.

Physical Science

Shadows

25

Shadows

Shadow Match

Draw a line to match.

shadow

glass

light

Finish the sentence.

When light cannot move through something,

it makes a _____.

Physical Science

What Made the Shadow?

Draw a line to match.

Shadow and Light Words

Read the words in the word box.
Find the hidden words. Circle them.

Word Box

shadow	light	glass	dark
through	shine	line	move

```
d  r  k  o  u  m  g  l  s  i
a  s  h  a  d  o  w  n  e  d
l  g  t  n  u  v  r  t  c  a
i  s  h  i  n  e  k  h  v  r
g  a  r  t  h  o  n  r  u  k
h  e  g  l  a  s  s  o  r  t
t  a  c  h  r  o  k  u  d  l
s  l  i  n  e  v  d  g  o  e
t  o  w  d  h  i  t  h  e  k
```

Shadows

Physical Science

Use Vocabulary

Finish each sentence.

| light | line | shadow |

1. Light moves in a _____.

2. _____ cannot move through some things.

3. A _____ is a dark spot.

Draw an object or person that has a shadow.

Shadow Art

Create a picture that has a shadow.

What You Need

- black, white, and light-colored construction paper
- crayons
- scissors
- glue

What You Do

1. Draw a picture of an object or person on the white paper.

2. Put the black piece of paper behind the white paper. Cut out your drawing.

3. Draw a sun on the light-colored construction paper. Glue your drawing onto the paper. Glue the shadow onto the paper.

4. Write a sentence that tells what the picture shows.

Shadows

Shadow Walk

Go outside and find shadows.

Skill:

Make scientific observations and record information

What You Need

- a camera

What You Do

1 On a sunny day, get a camera and go for a walk.

2 Look for shadows outside. When you see a shadow, take a picture of it.

3 After you get home, look through your pictures and answer the questions below.

Draw and write to answer the questions.

1. What shadow did you like best? Draw it.

```

```

2. What did it show? _____

3. Why was there a shadow? _____

_____

Shadows

Concept:

We use technology to communicate.

Technology

We use technology to read, play games, look and listen, and talk to each other. These things are technology.

computer

cellphone

tablet

television

People use technology to learn.

People use technology to have fun.

Physical Science

Technology

33

Skill:

Match graphic images to words

Tech Match

Draw a line to match.

cellphone

computer

television

tablet

Finish the sentence.

These things are _____.

Technology

Technology

Draw a line to match.

talk

play

learn

look and listen

Technology Words

Read the words in the word box.
Find the hidden words. Circle them.

Word Box

tablet	computer	television	cellphone
fun	play	learn	technology

```
c  m  p  o  t  f  u  n  r  l
t  e  l  e  v  i  s  i  o  n
a  l  e  a  r  n  t  v  e  m
b  f  u  l  y  p  h  o  e  p
l  c  o  m  p  u  t  e  r  l
e  l  l  g  y  c  a  m  r  a
t  f  n  o  u  t  e  v  n  y
c  e  l  l  p  h  o  n  e  r
t  e  c  h  n  o  l  o  g  y
```

Living or Not Living?

Level 2

Technology

Physical Science

Use Vocabulary

Skill:

Apply science vocabulary in context sentences

Finish each sentence.

learn	technology	talk

1. People use _____ to read.

2. People use technology to _____.

3. People use technology to _____ to each other.

Draw a picture of your favorite technology.

Technology

Skill:

Apply science concepts to real-world situations

Technology at Home

Does your family use technology at home? Draw 4 kinds of technology you use at home and write the names.

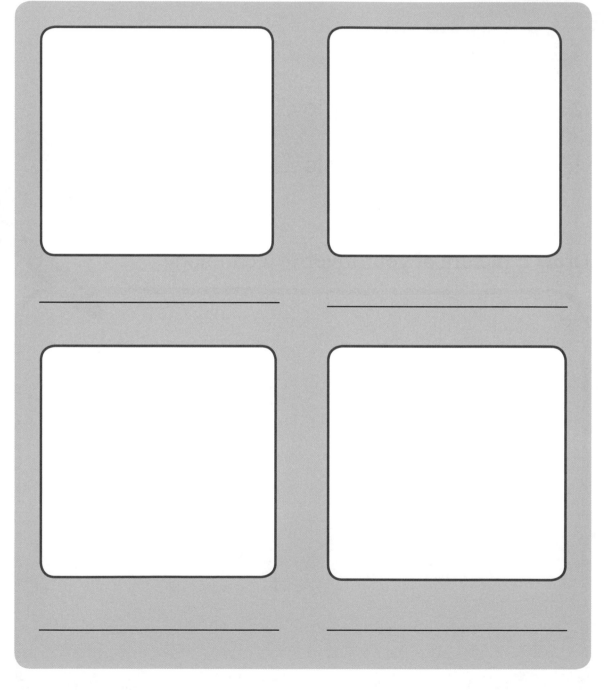

Technology

Physical Science

Technology at School

Does your school use technology?
Draw 4 kinds of technology you use
at school and write the names.

Skill:

Apply science
concepts to real-
world situations

Technology

Physical Science

Concept:

Leaves help trees survive and grow.

All Kinds of Leaves

Leaves help trees grow and live.
Trees grow leaves of many shapes
and sizes.

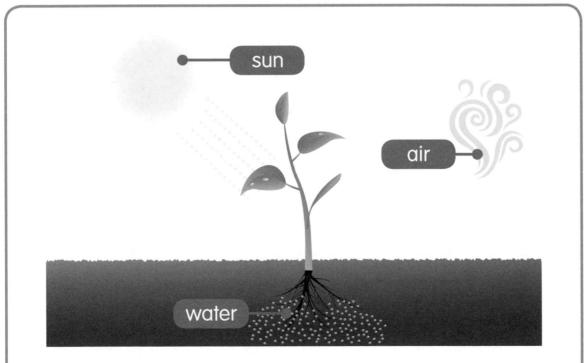

Leaves look different.

But they have the same parts.

Leaves make food for the tree. They make food from the sun, air, and water.

Leaves

Skill:

Label graphic images to demonstrate understanding of science concepts

Leaf Parts

Trace each word to label the leaf parts.

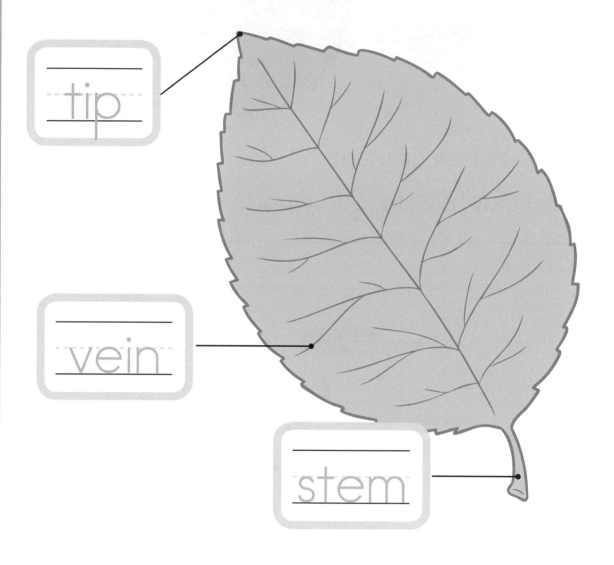

tip

vein

stem

Finish the sentence.

Leaves help trees grow and _____.

Leaves

Skill:
Visual discrimination

Leaves Have Shapes

Draw a line to match.

Leaf Words

Unscramble the words about leaves.
Write the words in the boxes.

Word Box

tip	leaf	tree	sizes
leaves	live	shapes	grow

sevale

fael

eret

izsse

ipt

viel

phesas

wogr

Use Vocabulary

Skill:

Apply science vocabulary in context sentences

Finish each sentence.

| trees | live | food |

1. Leaves help trees grow and _____.

2. _____ grow leaves of many shapes and sizes.

3. Leaves make _____ for the tree.

Draw your favorite leaf.

Life Science

Leaf Rubbings

Use real leaves to make a picture!

What You Need

- paper bag
- leaves of different shapes and sizes
- crayons with wrappers removed
- paper

Leaves

What You Do

1 Take the paper bag outdoors and collect leaves of different shapes, sizes, and colors.

2 On a hard, flat surface, place a leaf bottom side up on a piece of paper.

3 Put another sheet of paper on top of the leaf.

4 Rub the side of a crayon gently on the area over the leaf. Try to keep the leaf in place with one hand while you color with the other hand.

5 Do the same thing using other crayon colors and leaves.

6 Play with making patterns or your own "tree" of leaves.

Leaves

Animals and Eggs

Babies in Eggs

Some animals lay eggs. Their babies grow inside until they are ready to hatch.

bird

turtle

spider

snake

Animals with feathers, scales, or slippery skin lay eggs in many places.

Parents take care of their babies.

They feed them and keep them safe.

Life Science

Skill:

Match graphic images to words

Animals and Eggs

Egg Match

Draw a line to match.

turtle

spider

bird

snake

Finish the sentence.

Some animals hatch from _____.

Skill:

Label graphic images to demonstrate understanding of science concepts

A Life Cycle

Number the pictures to match.

1. The egg is layed.

2. The egg hatches.

3. The baby is fed.

4. The baby is kept safe.

Animals and Eggs

Life Science

Egg Words

Unscramble the words about eggs.
Write the words in the boxes.

Word Box

eggs	hatch	animals	babies
parents	feed	safe	lay

stepnar

gsge

chath

sabbei

aly

fase

malnisa

defe

Animals and Eggs

Use Vocabulary

Finish each sentence.

| parents | eggs | hatch |

1. Some animals lay _____.

2. Babies grow in the eggs until they _____.

3. _____ take care of their babies.

Draw an animal and its eggs.

Life Science   53

Skill: Apply science vocabulary in context sentences

Animals and Eggs

Animals and Eggs

What's Hatching Book

Make a book about animals that hatch from eggs!

What You Need

- scissors
- stapler
- crayons, colored pencils, or markers
- 3 sheets of white paper
- 1 sheet of construction paper

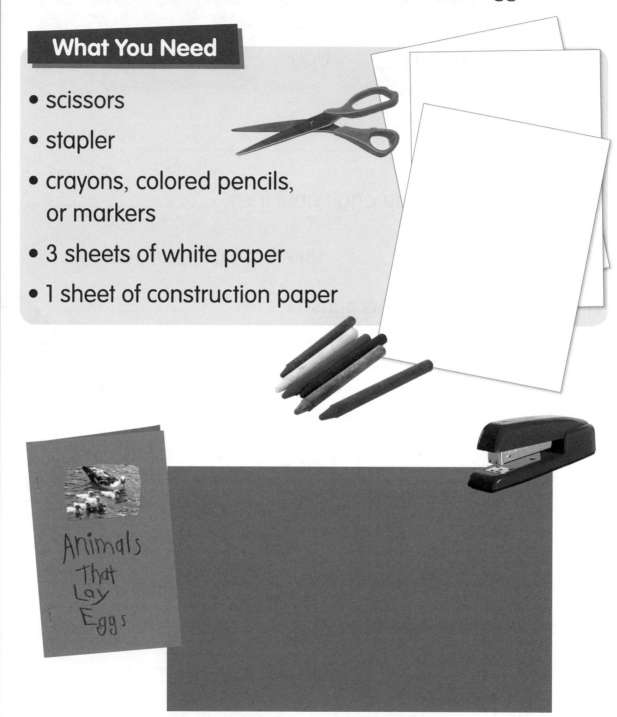

Animals That Lay Eggs

What You Do

1 Think about the animals that lay eggs.

2 Look at the pictures of the animals on pages 48–51 of this book.

3 Fold the sheets of white paper and construction paper in half. Staple the folded edge to make a book.

4 Cut out, from a magazine, a photo of an animal that lays eggs. Glue it to the cover of your book. Write a title for your book.

5 On each page of the book, draw a picture of an animal next to its baby hatching from an egg.

6 Write a sentence below each picture you draw.

7 Read your book to someone.

chickens lay eggs.

Animals and Eggs

Concept:

Some animal babies look like their mothers, but others do not.

Mothers and Babies

Some animal babies look
a lot like their mothers.

They have the same body parts.
They are the same color.
They are the same shape.

dog

puppy

Some babies do not look like
their mothers when they are born.
They look different.

butterfly

caterpillar

Life Science

Mothers and Babies

But they will grow and change.

One day, they will look like their mothers, too.

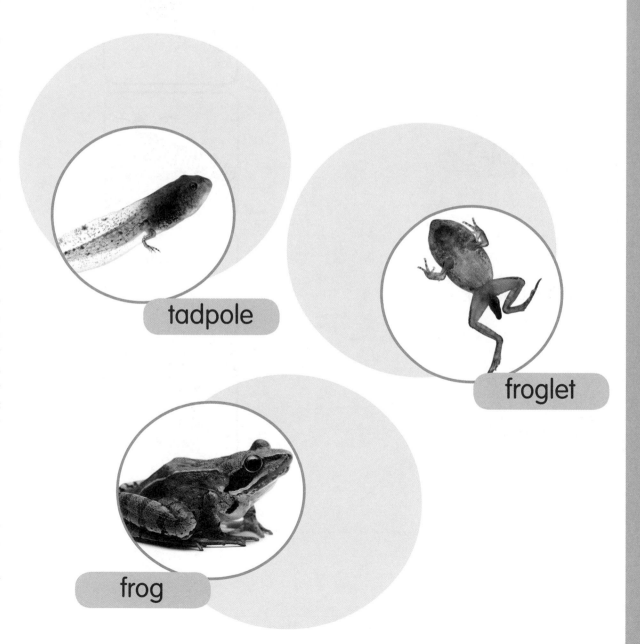

tadpole

froglet

frog

Life Science

Skill:

Match graphic images to words

Mothers and Babies

Baby Match

Draw a line to match.

puppy

tadpole

caterpillar

kitten

Finish the sentence.

Some animal babies look like their _____.

Animals Grow and Change

Draw a line to match.

Skill:
Match graphic images to demonstrate understanding of science concepts

Mothers and Babies

Mothers and Babies Words

Read the words in the word box.
Find the hidden words. Circle them.

Word Box

animal	babies	mothers	grow
change	born	butterfly	alike

c h a e t a r g l y

m f n b a b i e s e

o l i a b c g r o w

t a m o r i k e a l

h r a b r m o t n i

e g l u n c h a e m

r e y c h a l i k e

s b u t t e r f l y

c h a n g e b o r n

Use Vocabulary

Finish each sentence.

| babies | mothers | change | grow |

1. Some animal _____ look like their mothers.

2. Some animal babies do not look like their _____ when they are born.

3. Animal babies _____ and _____.

Draw a mother animal and her baby.

Life Science

Mothers and Babies

Mother and Baby

Draw a picture of a mother and her baby.

What You Need

- paper
- crayons or colored pencils

What You Do

mother   baby

The mother has wings and the baby has legs.

1 Choose an animal mother and baby to draw.

2 Draw a picture of the animal mother and her baby.

3 Write a sentence that tells how they are alike or different.

4 Show your picture to someone and explain how they are alike or different.

At the Pet Store

Visit a local pet store to see tadpoles and frogs.

Draw pictures of what you saw.

Tadpole	Frog

Write about what you saw.

_____

_____

_____

Mothers and Babies

Concept:

Animals have body parts that help them survive.

Birds of a Feather

Birds come in all colors, shapes, and sizes.

They have body parts that help them live.

Birds have feathers.

Feathers keep a bird warm.

Feathers also keep a bird dry.

Birds

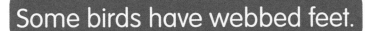
Some birds have webbed feet.

Webbed feet help birds swim.

Birds have beaks.

The shape of a bird's beak helps it eat.
Different birds have different beaks.

Birds are different from one another, but they
all have body parts that help them live.

Life Science

Parts of Birds

Draw a line to match.

feathers

webbed feet

long beak

Finish the sentence.

Birds have body parts that help them _____ .

Birds

Skill Sharpeners—Science • EMC 5321 • © Evan-Moor Corp.

Different Types of Beaks

Read the chart.

Type of Beak	What It Looks Like	What It's Used For
Spear beak		stabbing fish
Scoop beak		scooping fish out of water
Cracker beak		cracking seeds open

1. Which beak is used for scooping fish out of water?

   _____

2. Which beak is used for cracking seeds?

   _____

Skill:
Interpret information from charts or graphs

Bird Words

Read the words in the word box.
Find the hidden words. Circle them.

Word Box

birds	feathers	webbed	beaks
feet	swim	body	parts

```
w e b e a k s w e n
e f c h d a r p t s
h e m w e b b e d w
n a f e t r p o b i
d t b o d y a k f m
b h o y b b r a e t
b e s i f a t r e i
e r w m e h s b t r
p s e b i r d s o d
```

Use Vocabulary

Skill:

Apply science vocabulary in context sentences

Finish each sentence.

| webbed feet | feathers | shape |

1. Birds have _____ to keep them warm and dry.

2. Some birds have _____ .

3. The _____ of a bird's beak helps it eat.

Draw a bird using its beak to eat.

Bird Facts

Skill:

Do research to write and illustrate informational text

Learn more about your favorite bird.

What You Need

- paper
- crayons or colored pencils
- a book about birds, or a computer with an Internet connection

What You Do

1 Go to the library or use the Internet to learn more about birds.

2 Choose your favorite bird.

3 Find out:

◯ what it looks like
◯ where it lives
◯ what it eats
◯ how its body parts help it live

4 Draw and write about it on the next page.

bird's name

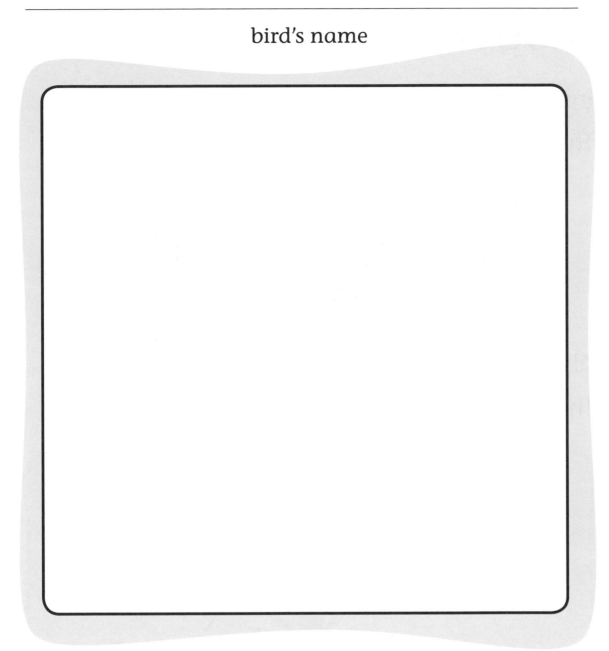

This bird's beak helps it _____.

This bird's wings help it _____.

This bird's feet help it _____.

Concept:

Insects are the same in many ways, but they are also different.

Insects

Insects are everywhere.

There are many different kinds of insects.

All insects have 3 body parts and 6 legs.

That is what makes them the same.

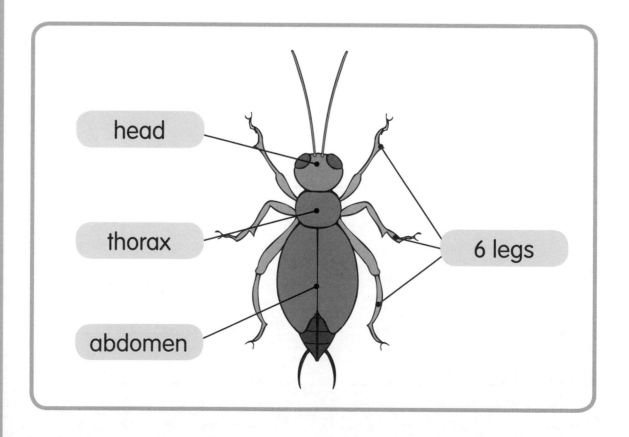

head

thorax

abdomen

6 legs

Insects

Insects look different from each other.

Insects move in different ways.

Some insects fly.

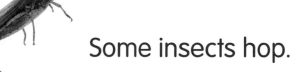

Some insects hop.

Some insects crawl.

Insect Match

Draw a line to match.

butterfly

ant

bee

grasshopper

Insects

Finish the sentence.

There are many different kinds of _____.

Life Science

Insect Parts

Trace the words.

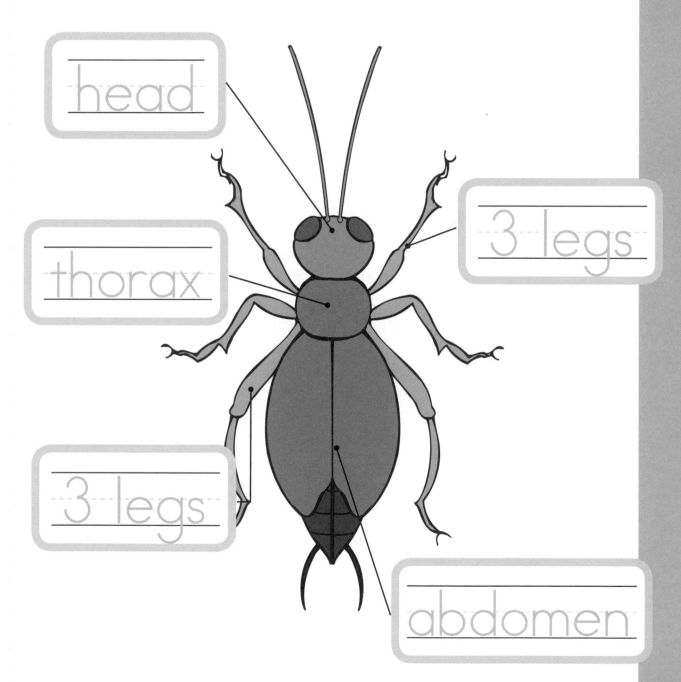

head

thorax

3 legs

3 legs

abdomen

Insects

Insect Words

Unscramble the words about insects. Write the words in the boxes.

Word Box

butterfly	moth	insect	wings
legs	body	ant	fly

thom

slge

lyf

tan

swnig

nestci

fylbertut

obyd

Life Science   Skill Sharpeners—Science • EMC 5321 • © Evan-Moor Corp.

Use Vocabulary

Finish each sentence.

| insects | butterflies | different |

1. All _____ have three body parts and six legs.

2. _____ and moths are insects.

3. Insects may look _____.

Draw an insect.

Insect Hunt

Go outside and look for insects. Make a check mark for each insect you find.

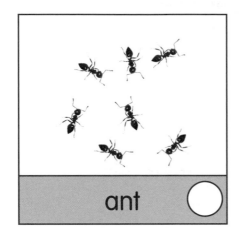

ant ◯

fly ◯

bee ◯

moth ◯

butterfly ◯

ladybug ◯

Insects

Life Science

Insect Book

Skill:

Make real-world observations and write about them

Make an insect book to read to someone.

What You Need

- 3 sheets of white paper
- 1 sheet of construction paper
- crayons, colored pencils, or markers
- stapler

What You Do

1 Think about the insects you saw on the insect hunt. Think about what each insect looks like and where you saw it.

2 Fold the sheets of paper and the construction paper in half. Staple the folded edge to make a book.

3 Cut out, from a magazine, a photo of an insect. Glue it to the cover of your book. Write a title for your book.

4 On each page of the book, draw a picture of a different insect and write a sentence about it.

5 After you are finished, read your book to someone.

Insects

The Night Sky

We see stars shining at night.

Stars make their own light.

We see the moon shining at night.

It does not make its own light.

Light from the sun makes

the moon shine bright.

sun

Earth

moon

The sun shines on the moon in different ways.
The part of the moon we can see changes.

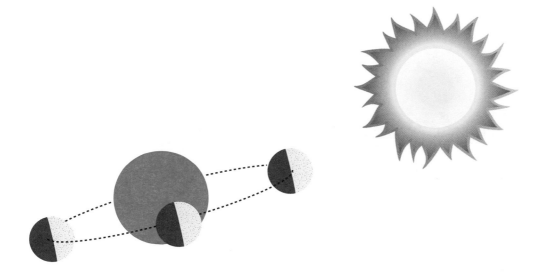

We call these changes the phases of the moon.

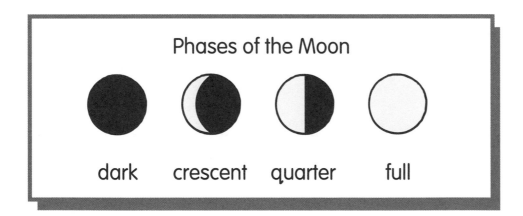

Night Sky

Skill:

Match graphic
images to words

Objects in the Sky

Draw a line to match.

star

full moon

sun

crescent moon

Finish the sentence.

The moon gets light from the _____.

Skill:

Match graphic images to science concepts

Moon Phases

Draw a line to match.

dark

cannot see the moon

quarter

can see half of the moon

full

can see all of the moon

crescent

can see a small part of the moon

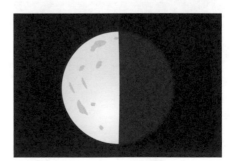

Night Sky

Skills:

Read science words; Visual discrimination

Night Sky Words

Unscramble the words about the night sky.
Write the words in the boxes.

Word Box

star	light	moon
sun	phases	shine

esshap

gilth

hisen

nus

omon

rast

Night Sky

Use Vocabulary

Finish each sentence.

| moon | light | sun |

1. Stars make their own _____.

2. Light from the _____ makes the moon shine bright.

3. The part of the _____ we can see changes.

Draw your favorite phase of the moon.

Night Sky

Space and Earth Science

Night Sky

Moon Art

Make pictures that show the phases of the moon!

What You Need

- 3 sheets of white paper
- 3 sheets of black paper
- 4 sheets of colored construction paper
- a bowl or round traceable object
- crayons
- scissors
- glue

What You Do

1 Set a bowl on a white sheet of paper. Trace around it. Cut it out. Do the same thing with each sheet of white paper.

2 Repeat Step 1 with the three sheets of black paper.

3 **Make a dark moon:** Glue a black circle to a piece of construction paper. Label it "dark moon."

4 **Make a crescent moon:** Cut a crescent shape out of a white circle. Glue it to a black circle. Glue it to the construction paper. Label it "crescent moon."

5 **Make a quarter moon:** Cut one black circle in half. Glue one half of it onto one full white circle. Glue it to the construction paper. Label it "quarter moon."

6 **Make a full moon:** Glue a white circle to a sheet of construction paper. Label it "full moon."

7 **Share it:** Put your pictures in order and tell someone about the phases of the moon.

Step 3   Step 4   Step 5   Step 6

Night Sky

Our Sun

The sun is a star .
It is far, far away.

The sun is so hot
that we can feel its heat .

The sun is so bright
that we can see its light .

Skill Sharpeners—Science • EMC 5321 • © Evan-Moor Corp.

The sun warms the land, air, and water.

Sunlight warms the earth for people, animals, and plants to live.

Sunlight makes plants grow.

People and animals need plants for food.

Without the sun, nothing could live on Earth.

Skill:

Match graphic
images to words

Sun Match

Draw a line to match.

sun

Earth

plants

animals

Finish the sentence.

The sun warms the land, air, and _____.

Our Sun

          Skill Sharpeners—Science • EMC 5321 • © Evan-Moor Corp.

Skill:
Match graphic images to words

The Sun

Label the things that need the sun.

land   water   plants   animals   people

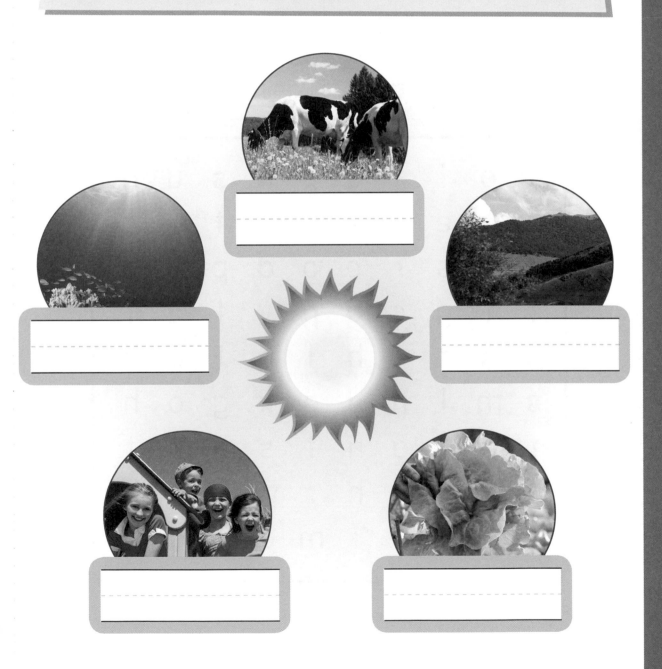

Our Sun

Sun Words

Read the words in the word box.
Find the hidden words. Circle them.

Word Box

heat	light	sun	earth
people	plants	animals	star

```
p o l i g p h s u n
a h e a t e s t r a
n m s r c o d p i n
i l g c b p v l a m
e a r t h l h i p e
s m l n d e k g o h
t p l a n t s h k t
a i k b h r w t a h
r o a n i m a l s p
```

Our Sun

Use Vocabulary

Skill:

Apply science vocabulary in context sentences

Finish each sentence.

| star | heat | warms |

1. The sun is a _____.

2. The sun is so hot that we can feel its
   _____.

3. The sun _____ the land, air, and water.

Draw the sun warming people and animals.

Our Sun

Skill:

Make real-world observations and write about them

Hot Rocks

The sun warms the land. Test it for yourself!

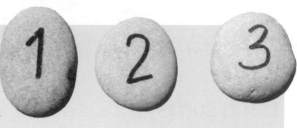

What You Need

• 3 rocks of the same kind

• a black permanent marker

What You Do

❶ Number each rock so that you will be able to identify it.

❷ Set the numbered rocks in 3 different areas.

Rock 1: a shaded spot indoors

Rock 2: a shaded spot outdoors

Rock 3: a sunny spot outdoors

❸ After one hour, feel each rock. Draw an X on the Heat Chart to tell how each rock felt.

❹ Then answer the questions about the rocks.

Our Sun

Heat Chart

Make an X to tell how each rock felt.

	Cold	Warm	Hot
Rock 1 shaded indoors			
Rock 2 shaded outdoors			
Rock 3 sunny outdoors			

1. Which rock felt the hottest?

_____

2. Why do you think that was?

_____

3. Which rock was the coolest?

_____

4. Why do you think that was?

_____

Our Sun

Concept:

Weather changes from season to season.

Seasons

Spring, summer, fall, and winter are seasons.

A season is a time of year.

Each season lasts three months.

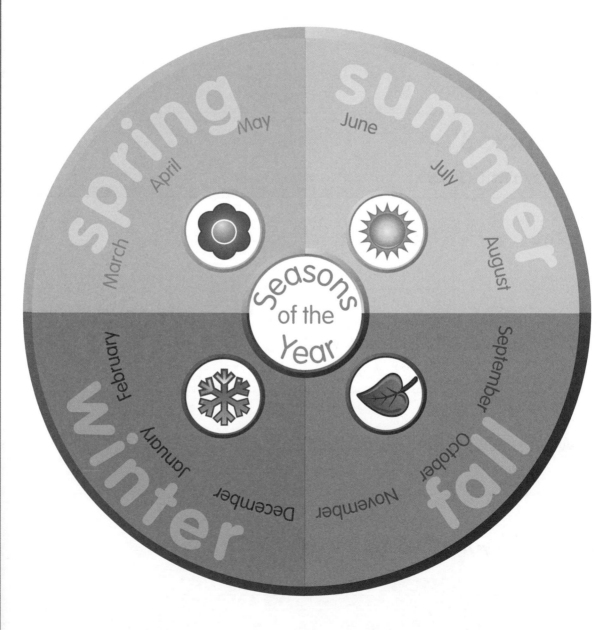

The weather changes each season.

Spring can be
warm and rainy.

Summer can be
hot and sunny.

Fall can be
cool and windy.

Winter can be
cold and snowy.

Then the pattern starts all over with spring!

Seasons

Season Match

Draw a line to match.

winter

spring

summer

fall

Finish the sentence.

A season is a time of _____.

Skill:

Match graphic images to science concepts

Season Names

Label each season. Draw a picture to tell about the weather.

winter   spring   summer   fall

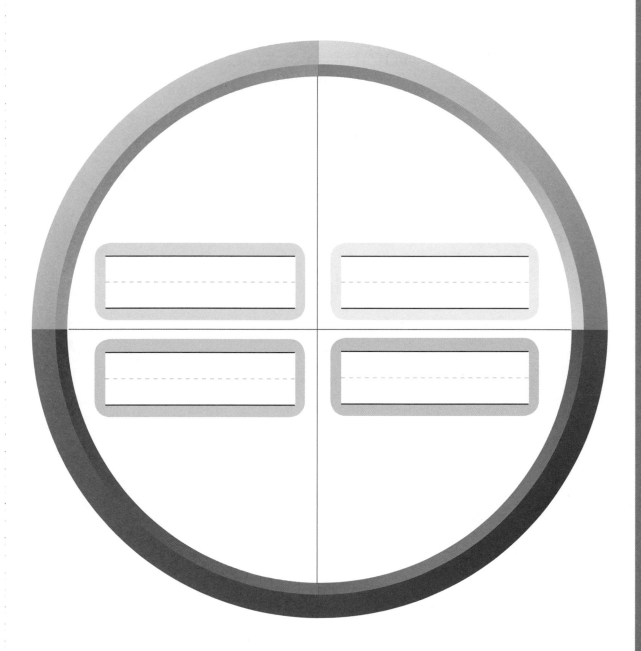

Season Words

Unscramble the words about the seasons.
Write the words in the boxes.

Word Box

summer	fall	spring	winter
season	warm	cold	hot

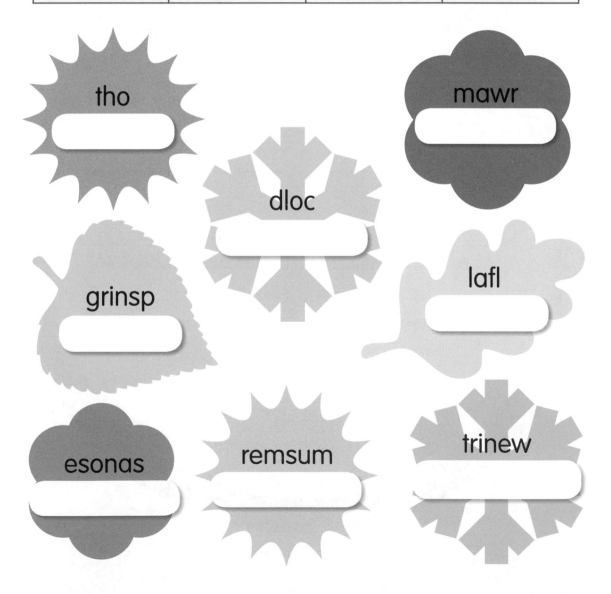

tho

mawr

dloc

grinsp

lafl

esonas

remsum

trinew

Seasons

Skill Sharpeners—Science • EMC 5321 • © Evan-Moor Corp.

Use Vocabulary

Finish each sentence.

weather	year	seasons

1. Spring, summer, winter, and fall are _____.

2. A season is a time of _____.

3. The _____ changes each season.

Draw a picture of a tree in the fall.

Fingerpaint Trees

Use your hands to make trees for four seasons.

- white paper
- colored construction paper
- paints

- scissors
- glue
- paper plates

What You Do

1 Cut 2 sheets of white paper in half to make four sheets.

2 Pour brown paint onto a paper plate. Dip your hand and your wrist into the paint and press your hand and wrist onto one sheet of white paper to make the tree trunk and branches.

3 Do the same thing on each sheet of white paper. Let your "trees" dry.

4 Pour small amounts of colored paints onto paper plates. Dip the tip of your finger into one color at a time and fingerpaint leaves on the trees for each season.

5 After your trees are dry, glue them to the construction paper in order of the seasons: spring, summer, fall, winter.

6 Write about your painting on the next page.

Seasons

The Four Seasons

Write about the weather and how the tree changed during each season in your painting.

Spring

weather: _____

tree: _____

Summer

weather: _____

tree: _____

Fall

weather: _____

tree: _____

Winter

weather: _____

tree: _____

Seasons

Wood Is Good

Trees give us wood. People use wood to build and make things.

We use things made from wood at home, at school, and around town.

Uses of Wood

Some things made
from wood are large,
some are small.

Some are used outdoors,
some are used indoors.

Some are for play, and
some are very important.

Even paper is made from wood!
We use wood every day.

Skill:

Match graphic images to words

Uses of Wood

Wood Match

Draw a line to match.

home

school

town

Finish the sentence.

We use wood to _____ things.

Which Is Wood?

Look at the items in each box.
Circle the one that is made from wood.

Skill:

Match graphic images to science concepts

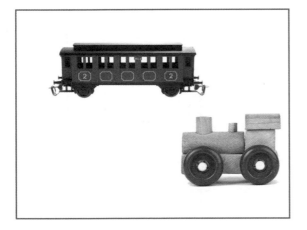

Uses of wood

Wood Words

Read the words in the word box.
Find the hidden words. Circle them.

Word Box

wood	build	trees	house
paper	school	town	table

```
m s c h o o l e e o
r c t r e a c c t w
p a p e r h t b a t
w d w c p a r h b l
b h o u s e e s l c
u n d w o r e n e m
i h t v k b s d c l
l e w o o d a i m r
d r i n c t o w n e
```

Uses of Wood

Use Vocabulary

Finish each sentence.

town	trees	build

1. _____ give us wood.

2. People use wood to _____ things.

3. Many things around home, school, and

   _____ are made of wood.

Draw something that you use that's made from wood.

USES of WOOD

Wood at Home

Look around your house and find things that are made from wood. Use the chart to show what the items are and how they are used.

1. Write the name of each item.

2. Draw a picture of the item.

3. Tell how you use the item.

Name of Item	What It Looks Like	How We Use It
pencil		to write with

Uses of Wood

I Use Wood to Make Things

Use wooden craft sticks to build something with wood.

What You Need

- wooden craft sticks
- paper and pencil
- glue
- paint (optional)

What You Do

1. Think of something you'd like to build with the craft sticks. Some ideas are a pencil or toothbrush holder, an ornament, or a napkin holder.

2. Draw a picture of what you'd like to make.

3. Use craft sticks and glue to make your item.

4. If you use natural colored sticks, you may want to paint your item.

5. After it dries, use it!

Uses of Wood

Earth Materials

We Use Materials

Earth has rocks, soil, and water. These are called earth materials . People, plants, and animals use earth materials to live.

Rocks have many different colors, sizes, and shapes. Some animals make their homes in rocks. People use rocks to build homes and buildings.

Soil has many different forms. Plants need soil to grow. Some animals need soil to build their homes.

Water is found in many places on Earth. People, plants, and animals need water to live. People use water to cook, clean, and do work.

Earth Materials

Earth Materials Match

Draw a line to match.

rocks

water

soil

Finish the sentence.

Soil, rocks, and water are called _____.

Earth Materials

What Is It?

Make an X on the one that doesn't belong.

Earth Materials

rocks

water

soil

Earth Materials Words

Read the words in the word box.
Find the hidden words. Circle them.

Word Box

water	soil	rock	plants
people	live	earth	materials

```
e m a t e r i a l s
a r w r o c k t h k
l w i v r s o i l p
p a h t p o r e k i
e t t v l e a r t h
o e w b a c m i c t
p r c h n a t w a l
l v r a t o l i v e
e i w c s m r a h i
```

Environment and Ecology Science   Skill Sharpeners—Science • EMC 5321 • © Evan-Moor Corp.

Use Vocabulary

Skill:

Apply science vocabulary in context sentences

Finish each sentence.

live	rocks	materials

1. Earth has soil, _____, and water.

2. These are called earth _____.

3. People, plants, and animals use earth materials

   to _____.

Draw an earth material you use.

Earth Materials

Earth Materials

How I Use Earth Materials

Look around your house, both indoors and outdoors, and find earth materials you use.

What You Do

1 Think about how you use these earth materials to help you do something.

2 Draw pictures and write about how you use each earth material on the next page.

How I Use Earth Materials

Draw a picture of how you use earth materials and write a sentence about it.

rocks

_____

_____

_____

water

_____

_____

_____

soil

_____

_____

_____

Earth Materials

Concept:

Recycling can reduce our impact on the environment.

Recycle and Reuse

Have you seen this?

It is on trash cans.

It is on bottles and cans.

It tells us to recycle or reuse .

We can recycle many things.

glass

plastic

paper

Some things are not easy to recycle. But you don't have to throw them away. You can reuse them in a different way.

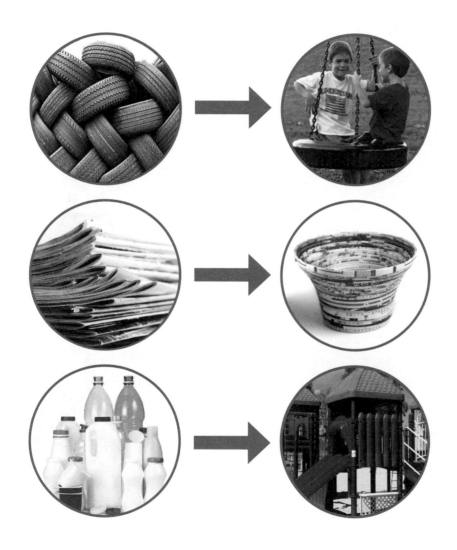

When we recycle or reuse things, we have less garbage. Having less garbage is good for Earth.

Recycle Match

Draw a line to match.

plastic

glass

paper

recycle

....

Finish the sentence.

This means _____.

Environment and Ecology Science   Skill Sharpeners—Science • EMC 5321 • © Evan-Moor Corp.

Things to Recycle

Draw a line to match. Put the materials in the correct recycle bin!

Skill:

Match graphic images to science concepts

Recycling Words

Unscramble the words about recycling.
Write the words in the boxes.

Word Box

recycle	reuse	garbage	cans
earth	glass	paper	plastic

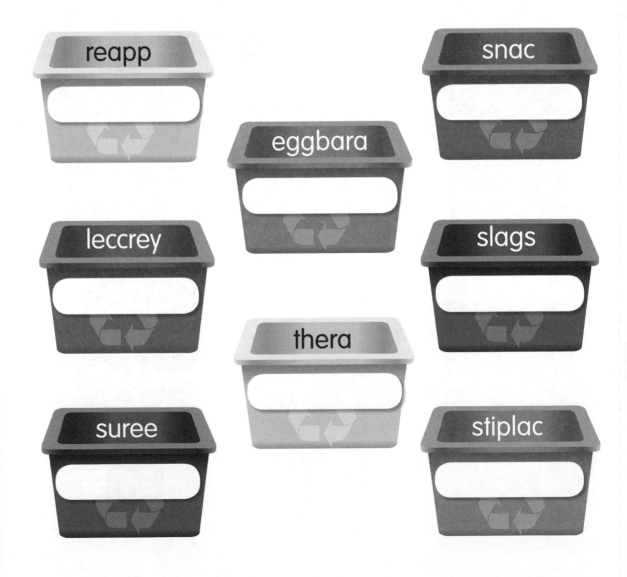

Environment and Ecology Science   Skill Sharpeners—Science • EMC 5321 • © Evan-Moor Corp.

Use Vocabulary

Skill:

Apply science vocabulary in context sentences

Finish each sentence.

| different | recycle | garbage |

1. We can _____ many things.

2. We can reuse things in _____ ways.

3. When we recycle or reuse things, we have less _____.

Draw things you recycle.

Recycling

Recycling

Birdfeeder

Reuse a milk carton to feed the birds in your backyard!

What You Need

- half-gallon milk carton
- knife (adult use only)
- hole punch
- paint
- paintbrush

- 5 or 6 thin sticks (twigs or chopsticks)
- glue
- stickers, buttons, or beads
- birdseed

What You Do

1 Rinse out the milk carton well. Dry it. Set the milk carton on a flat surface.

2 Ask an adult to cut out an opening in one side of the carton as shown.

3 Punch a hole below the opening.

4 Paint the outside of the carton. After the paint dries, decorate the carton so it looks like it has flowers on it. Use stickers or glue buttons or beads onto it.

5 Ask an adult to cut the thin sticks into halves. Glue the sticks along both topsides of the carton to create a roof.

6 Place a long stick through the hole to make a perch. Glue the end of the stick to the inside back of the carton.

7 Fill the feeder with birdseed and place it outside.

8 Watch the birds use your reused milk carton as a feeder!

Recycling

Concept:
The shape and design of a tool are related to its function.

The Best Tool for the Job

A **tool** is an item we use to do a job.
Tools have different **shapes** to help us
do different jobs.

Straws help us sip.

Scissors help us cut.

Ladles help us scoop.

Engineering and Design   Skill Sharpeners—Science • EMC 5321 • © Evan-Moor Corp.

Shovels help us dig.

Funnels help us pour.

Look around your house.
Notice the tools you use and how their
special shapes help you do different jobs.

Engineering and Design

Tool Match

Skill:

Match graphic
images to words

Draw a line to match.

scissors

shovel

ladle

straw

Finish the sentence.

The shape of each tool helps it do its _____.

Engineering and Design   Skill Sharpeners—Science • EMC 5321 • © Evan-Moor Corp.

The Best Tool for the Job

Circle the tool that would be best for each job.

Skill:

Match graphic images to science concepts

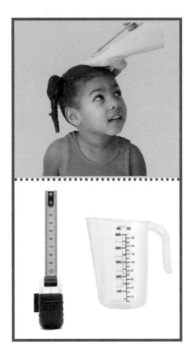

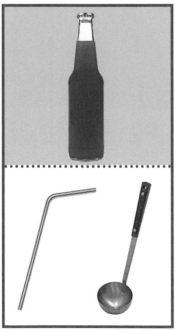

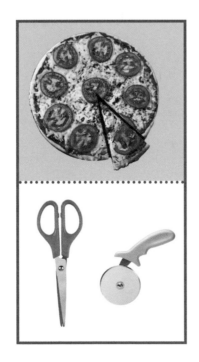

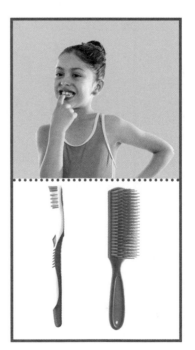

Tools

Tool Words

Read the words in the word box.
Find the hidden words. Circle them.

Word Box			
tool	shape	job	different
straw	scissors	shovel	ladle

o	d	i	n	s	h	o	l	r	p
u	i	j	o	b	b	f	f	a	r
h	f	s	t	n	s	h	a	p	e
t	f	s	c	i	s	s	o	r	s
o	e	c	s	o	d	i	b	a	d
o	r	t	t	s	h	o	v	e	l
l	e	c	r	s	y	a	h	f	r
h	n	d	a	l	a	d	l	e	e
a	t	h	w	a	p	e	f	j	o

Use Vocabulary

Skill:

Apply science vocabulary in context sentences

Finish each sentence.

| tool | helps | shape |

1. A _____ is an item you use to do a job.

2. Each tool _____ you do different things.

3. The _____ of each tool helps it do its job.

Draw a picture of a tool that you use every day.

Paper Funnel Tool

Make a paper funnel and try it out!

What You Need

- 1 sheet of paper (any kind)
- scissors
- tape

What You Do

1 Cut a circle shape out of a piece of paper. It does not have to be a perfect circle.

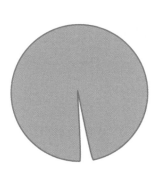

2 From the outside edge, cut a slit to the center of the circle.

3 Slide one of the cut edges over the other. Continue to slide each of the cut edges opposite one another. Tape the outside edge so that it keeps its shape.

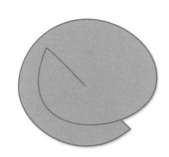

4 Cut the tip to create an opening. The size of the opening depends on what you will be funneling through it.

Tools

I Made a Tool

Tell about the paper funnel you made and how you used it.

I made a _____.

I used it to _____

_____.

The _____ made work easier because

it helped me _____

_____.

Draw what you poured into your funnel, and the container that you poured it into.

This is how I used my paper funnel.

Engineering and Design

Tools

Answer Key

Page 10

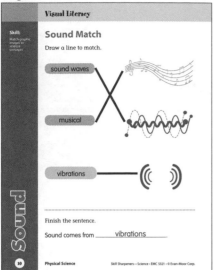

Page 11

Page 12

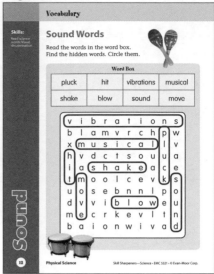

Page 13

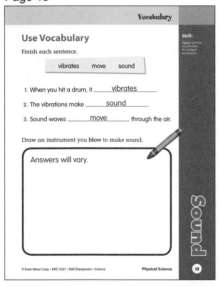

Page 15

Page 18

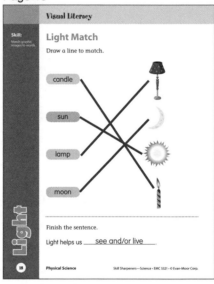

Page 19

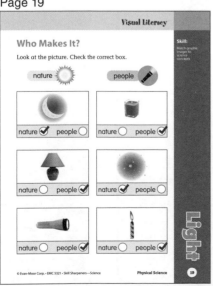

Page 20

Page 21

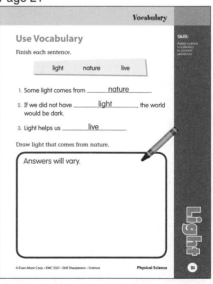

Page 22

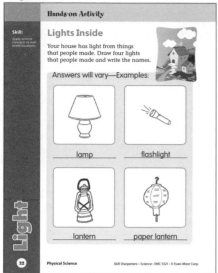

Page 23

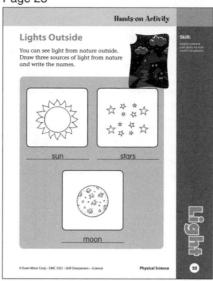

Page 26

Page 27

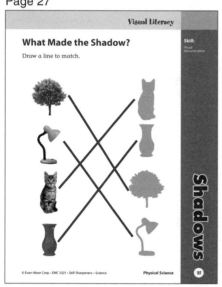

Page 28

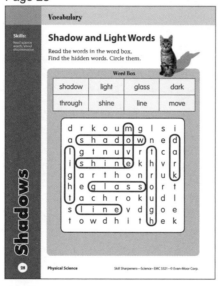

Page 29

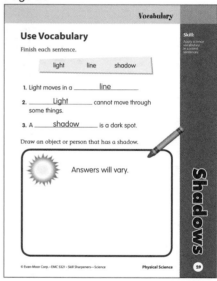

Page 31

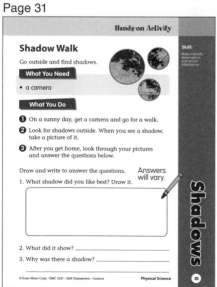

Page 34

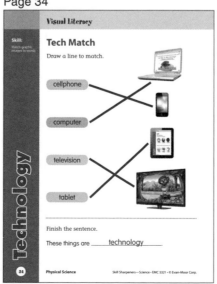

Page 35

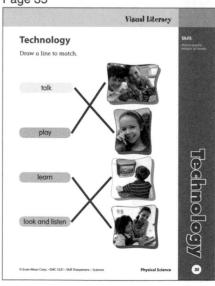

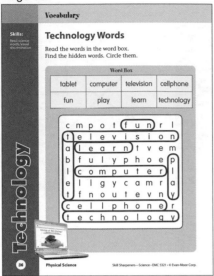

Vocabulary

Technology Words

Read the words in the word box.
Find the hidden words. Circle them.

Word Box

| tablet | computer | television | cellphone |
| fun | play | learn | technology |

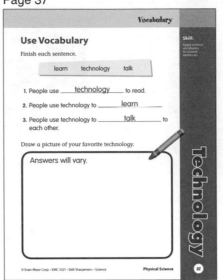

Vocabulary

Use Vocabulary

Finish each sentence.

learn   technology   talk

1. People use ___technology___ to read.
2. People use technology to ___learn___
3. People use technology to ___talk___ to each other.

Draw a picture of your favorite technology.

Answers will vary.

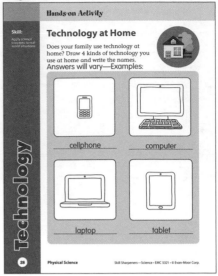

Hands-on Activity

Technology at Home

Does your family use technology at home? Draw 4 kinds of technology you use at home and write the names.
Answers will vary—Examples:

cellphone   computer
laptop   tablet

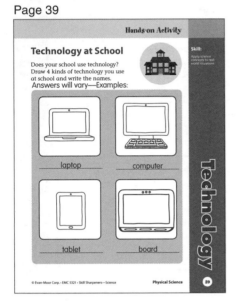

Hands-on Activity

Technology at School

Does your school use technology? Draw 4 kinds of technology you use at school and write the names.
Answers will vary—Examples:

laptop   computer
tablet   board

Visual Literacy

Leaf Parts

Trace each word to label the leaf parts.

tip
vein
stem

Finish the sentence.
Leaves help trees grow and ___live___

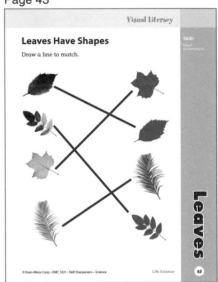

Visual Literacy

Leaves Have Shapes

Draw a line to match.

Vocabulary

Leaf Words

Unscramble the words about leaves.
Write the words in the boxes.

Word Box

| tip | leaf | tree | sizes |
| leaves | live | shapes | grow |

sevale — leaves
fael — leaf
eret — tree
izsse — sizes
ipt — tip
viel — live
phesas — shapes
wogr — grow

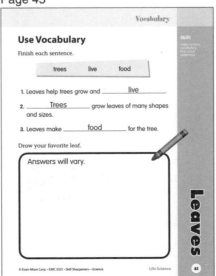

Vocabulary

Use Vocabulary

Finish each sentence.

trees   live   food

1. Leaves help trees grow and ___live___
2. ___Trees___ grow leaves of many shapes and sizes.
3. Leaves make ___food___ for the tree.

Draw your favorite leaf.

Answers will vary.

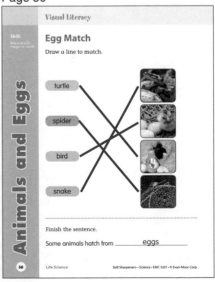

Visual Literacy

Egg Match

Draw a line to match.

turtle
spider
bird
snake

Finish the sentence.
Some animals hatch from ___eggs___

138   **Answer Key**

Page 51

A Life Cycle

Number the pictures to match.

1. The egg is layed.
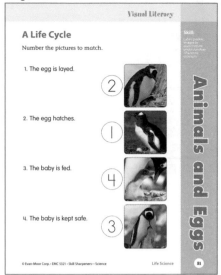 2

2. The egg hatches.
1

3. The baby is fed.
4

4. The baby is kept safe.
3

Animals and Eggs

Page 52

Egg Words

Unscramble the words about eggs.
Write the words in the boxes.

Word Box

eggs	hatch	animals	babies
parents	feed	safe	lay

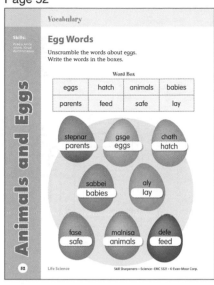

stepnar — parents
gsge — eggs
chath — hatch
sabbei — babies
aly — lay
fase — safe
malnisa — animals
defe — feed

Animals and Eggs

Page 53

Use Vocabulary

Finish each sentence.

parents	eggs	hatch

1. Some animals lay ___eggs___
2. Babies grow in the eggs until they ___hatch___
3. ___Parents___ take care of their babies.

Draw an animal and its eggs.

Answers will vary.

Animals and Eggs

Page 58

Baby Match

Draw a line to match.

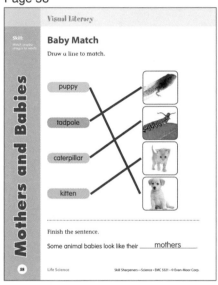

puppy
tadpole
caterpillar
kitten

Finish the sentence.
Some animal babies look like their ___mothers___

Mothers and Babies

Page 59

Animals Grow and Change

Draw a line to match.

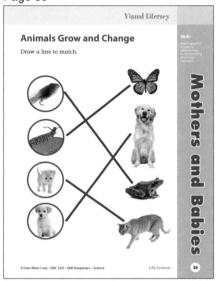

Mothers and Babies

Page 60

Mothers and Babies Words

Read the words in the word box.
Find the hidden words. Circle them.

Word Box

animal	babies	mothers	grow
change	born	butterfly	alike

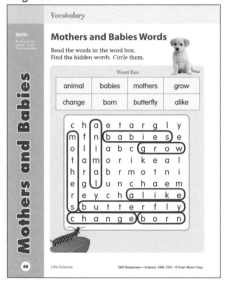

Mothers and Babies

Page 61

Use Vocabulary

Finish each sentence.

babies	mothers	change	grow

1. Some animal ___babies___ look like their mothers.
2. Some animal babies do not look like their ___mothers___ when they are born.
3. Animal babies ___grow___ and ___change___

Draw a mother animal and her baby.

Answers will vary.

Mothers and Babies

Page 63

At the Pet Store

Visit a local pet store to see tadpoles and frogs.

Draw pictures of what you saw.

Tadpole
Drawings will vary but should show at least one tadpole.

Frog
Drawings will vary but should show at least one frog.

Write about what you saw.

Answers will vary—Example: I saw tadpoles swimming in water and frogs sitting on rocks.

Mothers and Babies

Page 66

Parts of Birds

Draw a line to match.

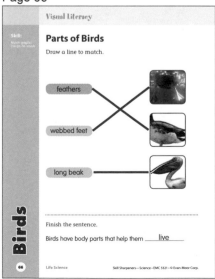

feathers
webbed feet
long beak

Finish the sentence.
Birds have body parts that help them ___live___

Birds

Page 67

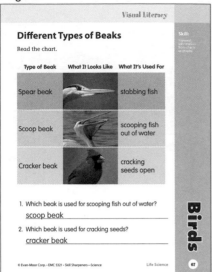

Page 68

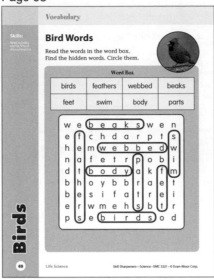

Page 69

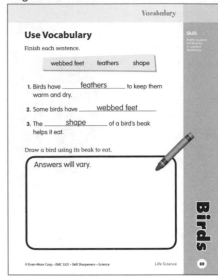

Page 71

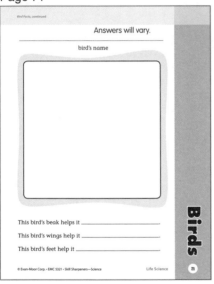

Page 74

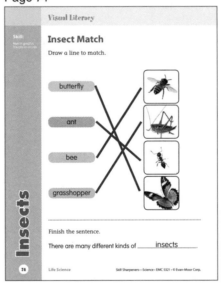

Page 75

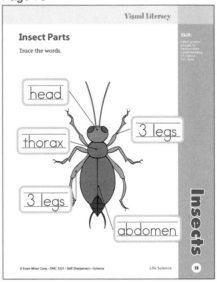

Page 76

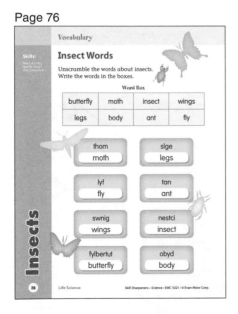

Page 77

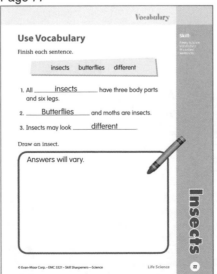

Page 82

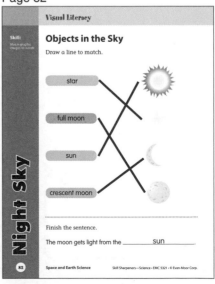

Page 83

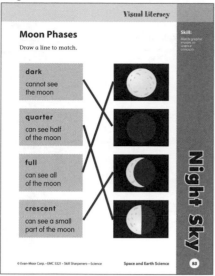

Page 84

Page 85

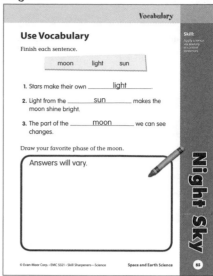

Page 90

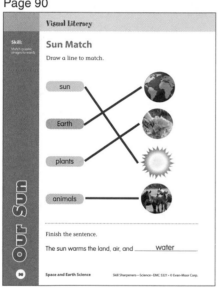

Page 91

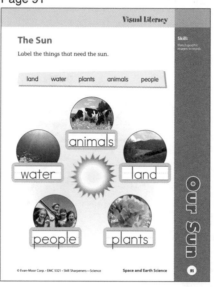

Page 92

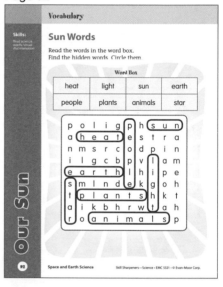

Page 93

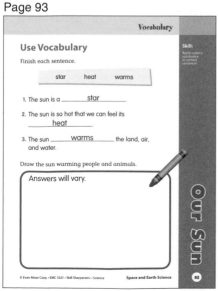

Page 95

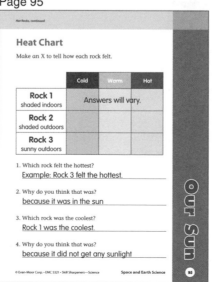

Page 98

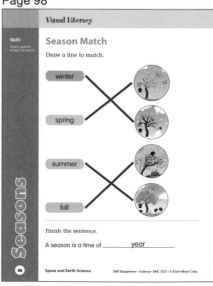

Page 99

Page 100

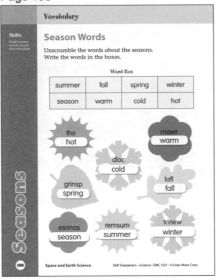

Page 101

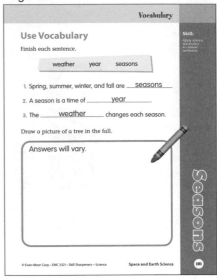

Page 103

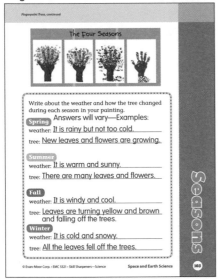

Page 106

Page 107

Page 108

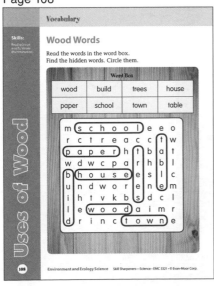

Page 109

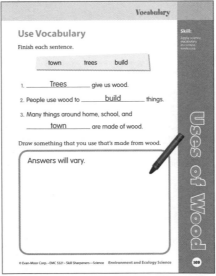

Page 110